HELP MONEY PROBLEMS

"45 TIPS AND TRICKS TO SAVE MONEY"

Wherever you find yourself on your financial journey, it is essential to know that it is possible for everyone to change their financial life and start saving money. Though some of the times it can be difficult at the beginning, but what you need to get started is the first step in the right direction. By doing this; the odds will favor you.

This is the primary aim of writing this book titled *"TIPS AND TRICKS TO SAVE MONEY"*. Though the fact is that none of the tips mentioned in this book are life-changing on their own, but they have been found to make a massive difference as time goes on in the event that you are able to utilize some of these tips. Some are not easy to practice, while some of them take a few minutes. When you do, you will soon realize that you are saving more than you ever thought possible. But overall, they are exceptionally simple - anyone can do them.

TIPS AND TRICKS TO SAVE MONEY

1. Pen down your expenses

One of the critical steps you need to take to ensure you are saving money is to determine how much you spend. Monitor all of your expenses; this includes and not limited to every coffee, homewares, and cash tip. As soon as you have all your data, place the numbers in the category they belong, such as gas, groceries, and mortgage, and add up each amount. To get an accurate amount, you can use your credit card bank statements and don't forget.

2. Move bank accounts to enjoy the benefits and earn more interest

In the event that you are charged a monthly fee for checking your account or savings account, it might be helpful to look for some of the available latest banking offers. Some of the best banks not only offer sign-up bonuses just to open an account and deposit directly, but some also offer attractive interest rates to new clients. You can also build an emergency fund; this can make a huge impact. Families on a low income of at least $500 in an emergency fund have better financial income than moderate-income families with less saved up.

3. Budget for savings

As soon as you get the exact figure of the amount of money you spent in a month, you can start to put in order your recorded expenses into a sustainable budget. Your budget should show how your expenses match your income, so you can plan your expenses and reduce the rate at which you spend. Be sure to consider expenses that happen regularly, but not every month, a good example is car maintenance. Try to include a savings category and save 10 to 15% of your income.

4. Find ways to reduce your spending

It can be difficult for you to have savings if your expenses are too high. Cutting back is another problem. All you need to do is to highlight those things that are not necessary, such as entertainment and dining out which consume high percent of your money. Also, try everything within your reach to save on your fixed monthly expenses such as television and mobile. Below are some useful tips that can help you cut your daily expenses:

- You can use community event listings to search for free or low-cost events in other to reduce the amount of money you spend on entertainment.
- Put an end to any form of subscriptions and memberships

you don't use, especially if they are subjected to the automatic renewal.

- Buy food outside just once in a month and anytime you are doing so make sure that you visit places where the prices are affordable.
- Try to cool yourself when you see things that can tempt you to overspend.

5. Set savings goals

If you are determined to save money, it is advisable to set a goal. And also think about what you could save for. It can be getting married, planning for a vacation, or saving for retirement. Then determine how much money you will need and how long it will take to save for it.

6. Decide on your priorities

After expenses and your income, your goals are likely to have the most significant impact on the distribution of savings. Remember your long-term goals: Short-term needs mustn't neglect retirement planning. When your saving goals are prioritized, this will make it easy for you to have a clear idea of where to start saving. Take for instance; in the event that you know the chance of getting new car next year is high, you can start saving money for one now.

7. Budget with money and envelopes

Sometimes you might face issues with overspending, at this time, trying the envelope budget system can be the best thing for you. With the envelope budgeting, you will be able to set an amount of cash for most of your expenses. And once the money is gone, it's gone.

8. Don't just save money, save for yourself

There is a vast difference between saving money for yourself and saving money for your future. So, you don't need to spend less, all you need to do is to put money into a savings account to plan for future expenses such as university expenses, retirement or emergencies that could help you improve financially.

9. Save automatically

Configuring automatic savings is the simplest and most efficient way to save money. It also allows you to lose sight of extra cash and out of your mind. This is how it works; on every payout, let your employer deduct a certain amount from your paycheck and wire it to a retirement or savings account. If you don't know much about this, you can ask your HR representative for details on how to set one up. Or at the end of every month, you can ask your bank or credit union to transfer a fixed amount from your checking account to your savings or investment account.

10. Turn off the television

An effective way to save money is to reduce the number of television shows you watch dramatically. A lot of financial benefits have been attributed to this: do not spend much on advertisements, cut your electric bill, devote more time to focus on other meaningful things in life such as business, etc.

11. Start selling something

A lot of people get it wrong then they think that collections are the secret to wealth. A lot of billionaires, today all over the world, sells one thing or the other. Beanie Babies was at one time a big fad craze at the time; the same thing applies to Longaberger baskets. Presently most of their items are available on resale sites, such as Craigslist and at garage sales for a fraction of their original cost, and many people who have made thousands of dollars in their "investments" are wondering what happened.

If you don't want such a relationship to happen, avoid collecting items that are of dubious value. If you want to recover some of the money you have already spent on collectibles, you can start selling them and use the money for other valuable financial goals.

12. Join as many free customer rewards program as possible

Irrespective of where you reside, there will be a number of retailers who are willing to reward you for shopping at their stores. The basic game plan you need to utilize this program is creating a Gmail or Yahoo address just for those messages; collect all the cards you can, then look for additional coupons in your account every time you're ready to buy. You can add to these rewards and discounts with rewards credit cards to earn points on purchases from a wide variety of stores that can be used to cashback or for other benefits.

13. Make your own gifts instead of buying things in the store.

If you want to save money while also giving out to people, these two goals can be accomplished by creating your own homemade gifts. Some of the things you can make easily and at a lower cost at home include food mixes, candles, fresh-baked or cookies, and soap, among other things.

These are spectacular gifts for others because they involve a personal touch - something you can't buy in the store - and are often consumable; this indicates that they won't end up stuffing someone's closet with junk, to be on a safer side you can put a personal handwritten note with the gift.

14. Master the 30-day rule

One of the most vital rules of personal finance is avoiding instant gratification, and in other to implement this rule, you need to wait for 30 days. Very often, after a month, you will find that your desire to buy is also gone and you will save money in the meantime. In any case, if you are about to make a purchase, a moment of waiting can give you a better idea of the value of your purchase;

15. Write a list before you go shopping - and stick to it.

One of the easiest ways to save money is to buy only when you have a list. Because when you have them, you usually end up with impulsive purchases and unplanned purchases - all of which cost money.

Creating a list before going to the grocery store is especially important. Not only can this help you buy items that are right for your meal, but you also avoid buying food that you might lose. Always create a list; this is important and sticks to it first. You can also take advantage of a cashback card that offers cash bonuses in stores and groceries, just make sure to pay your balance every month.

16. Invite friends to your house rather than going out

Going out to eat has a massive effect on your food budget, and it also affects your entertainment budget all at once. And anyway, it's always cheaper to stay with friends and organize your own party. Instead of going to town, have a fun introductory dinner with your friends. Play cards, sit around the fire pit, or watch movies with your guests. You will save money and at the end; you will have fun.

17. Repair turned clothes instead of throwing them away

Do not abandon a cloth because of a broken button; sew a new one with a very well-coordinated thread. Do not throw away your pants over holes, put them in a patch of some sort and save them for times when you are working around the house. Sewing is not a difficult task, it's something anyone can do, and a little bit of practice goes a long way.

18. Don't spend a lot of money to entertain your kids

Many kids, especially the younger ones, can have fun at a lower cost. You can buy them an end roll of newspaper from your local paper and allow them to exercise their creativity. Allow them to play ball in the backyard, take them to the park, you can plant a garden. Teach them to ride a bike without a training wheel once and for all. Understand that what your children want above all else is your time, not your job and that you will find money in your pockets and joy in your heart.

19. Watch your savings grow

Monitor your budget and watch how it grows monthly. This will not only help you adhere to your personal savings plan but also help you quickly identify and solve many problems. Having a better understanding of how to save money can be an added advantage which will inspire you to find more ways to save and achieve your goals faster.

20. Discuss rates with your credit card company or complete a balance transfer

In the event that you have been paying huge interest on your credit cards, it is high time to understand that you are in possession of some power so far you have been making your payments. Not only are you entitled to negotiate your current interest rate with your credit card issuer, but you also have the right to transfer your balance to a completely different card. (In fact, that may be your greatest asset.)

You can begin by putting a call through to your card issuer through the number on the back of your card and explaining your request. In the event that there has been no progress with them, try checking out the balance transfer credit cards to find one with an introductory 0% APR that could save you hundreds of dollars in interest as time goes on.

21. Clean out those closets

Browse your closets and find everything you no longer use. Then don't just get rid of it, use it to your advantage. You can have a yard sale with it which you can sell on eBay or Craigslist, put it in a shipment or even donate it for a tax deduction (write down what you give to get a receipt). All of these options can turn old items that you no longer want to cash in your pocket. Not only that, it is often a psychic burden to clean your closet.

22. Drink more water

Drinking lots of water has not only significant health benefits but also financial benefits. Drink a full glass of water before each meal to stay full and eat less. Not only will you save on your food bill, but you will also feel better after being adequately hydrated.

Better yet, consuming more water - in a reusable bottle or in a restaurant -

means spending less on drinks like soda, juice, and tea. Remember: tap water is not only as pure as bottled water; you will also get it without spending a penny.

22. Stay away from convenience foods and fast food

Instead of eating fast food or just eating a pre-cooked dinner when you get home, try making simple, healthy substitutes that you can bring with you. An hour's worth of preparation one weekend can leave you with a ton of cheap and easy dinner and snack options for the following week.

You can also consider breaking out the ol' crock pot as a replacement for an inexpensive meal option this helps to save money and time. In times when you just can't avoid eating, maximize your savings with coupons and a rewards credit card that gives you a bonus for restaurant costs (but you know better, so just spend it knowing you can pay every month without interest).

23. Stay away from smoking

It is high time for you to know that your smoking habit is not only expensive but can be a threat to your life. Putting an end to smoking will not only increase your life span but also save you a lot of money. Try some of the many available anti-smoking products, or switch to an electronic cigarette to save time. Whichever one you choose, you will be much better off.

24. Exchange some items such as books, music, and DVDs on the Internet or in the library.

It is very easy to swap/exchange books, CDs and DVDs you do not like online. What you need to do is to clean up your media collection and trade them with others online by making use of websites like Paperback Swap. Also, it becomes easy for you when you live close to a library that loan DVDs in addition to books. You will have a higher chance of saving more money if you can trade a lot with all these items.

25. Buy quality devices that will last

There are lots of benefits in taking time to do enough research when trying to buy a new appliance. Even when a reliable, energy-efficient washer and dryer could cost you a lot, but as time goes on, it saves you energy when it last for over 15 years instead of five, besides, you keep more money.

26. Make a price comparison - and locate a cheaper grocery store

A lot of people just get into a grocery store without even thinking about the price of the goods they have. But the good news is that there are a number of simple ways to find stores that sell goods at a cheaper rate. What you need to do is to keep a record of the ten items you buy most, then visit another shop for similar items and compare the price. Eventually, one shop will offer these items at low and affordable prices, and you will automatically save money.

27. Do not spend under stress

It is easy to justify spending money just to relax after a hard day's work. However, it is rarely a good idea. Instead of buying things you don't need to feel better; it might be wise to find other ways to relax. In this case, exercise becomes the best option. There are some things you can do to get relieved from stress, such as watching movies or do some things in your backyard.

28. Buy a new car and / or home insurance

If you have a car or a home, insurance is almost given, and you want to secure the best deal for your needs. It can be helpful to buy new car insurance or home insurance policy every few years to secure the best deal.

29. Stick to reliable and economical cars

Your mind will be at rest when you buy a reliable and fuel-efficient car. This is because you spend less on fuels and maintenance. Take for instance, if you choose a car that gets 15 miles per gallon over another car that gets 10, a lot of gas will be saved in this process.

30. Take note of the 10-second rule

When you visit a shop and add some items to your cart, try and pause for 10 seconds and ask yourself why you are buying it and whether you really need it or not. In the event that you can't provide a reasonable answer, return the item this will save you more money because you do not buy things that are not needed.

31. Give out free space in your home for rent

If you have unused space in your home, such as a bedroom or in-law suite, you can register on sites such as Airbnb.com and rent it out. You also earn more income if you live close to a popular or tourist area, you could make a lot of extra money. Just be sure you know the risks and are ready to take the necessary steps to protect your family and property.

32. Work on debt repayment

High-interest debt, such as credit cards, can backfire on your monthly income. You may be surprised at the amount of interest you pay each month if you keep your credit card balance. Paying off your credit cards as soon as possible will free up extra money in your budget and allow you to do more with your money. If you want to be more comfortable and save, it's essential to get rid of your debt.

33. Keep paying for your daily expenses with cash

Though it is not mandatory to pay rents or utility bills in cash, switching to cash for party expenses and paying grocery bill can help reduce the rate at which you spend. It is helpful to limit your costs strictly, and if you do not lower your debit card when making a purchase, you will be more aware of what you are spending. This can mean deciding on the store to put things in place, but it will also help you determine the best way to use the money you have because you will prioritize the money you spend on your purchases.

34. Find a way to cut big costs

Spend time to examine your total budget. Do you pay much for your car? Can you get new locations where the cost of living is low? Can you bring in roommates to lower the amount of money you spend on accommodation?

Though these could be the last steps to take when looking for ways to increase your savings but the fact and good news that accompany is that at the end of the month you save a reasonable amount of money. The lower your cost is, the easier it is to meet your budget. If you decide to sell your car, be sure to manage it properly and get a new and more reliable older car.

35. Find happiness in life, not spending

People often buy things because they think (unknowingly maybe) that it will bring them joy. They just have to have the latest gadget or shoes or cars. That's so much fun! Yet you buy such things and are only happy for a day or two. Then, you just need to buy more. It's an endless cycle. Instead, learn to love life. Find joy in nature! In the people around you! Doing something you love! In Exercise and Meditation! There are a lot of things we can do in life, which will make us happy, most of the times you don't need to spend before getting them.

36. Try frugal gift-giving.

Giving gifts to people is one of the most beautiful traditions because it shows generosity and friendliness. Until it becomes marketed; so it's costly. Instead, try giving the gift of spending time with someone. You can provide them with something you cooked or made yourself. Try to provide them with services that would cost you. You don't have to be expensive to be generous.

37. Spend enough time indoor

If you go out, you are more likely to spend unnecessarily. You spend a lot of money when you enter a restaurant to but food, go to the mall for shopping, stop at a gas station for a snack. To avoid this reckless spending, stay home, and find free entertainment. This is also one of the best ways to spend nice time with family and friends.

38. Eat breakfast

When you eat healthy breakfast, you become full for long and gain more energy during the day. This will reduce your urge to buy a big and expensive lunch. During this time, breakfast can be very healthy, fast, and cheap. A bowl of oatmeal in the morning is one of those things that can prevent you from rushing to eat an expensive lunch later in the day.

39. Learn to dress as simple as you can

Buy different shorts of simple clothes that fit you well; there is no need to get many clothes. Having a few pants, five shirts and five ties that work well is enough for you;

40. Discover free events in town

Some cities have beautiful parks, free basketball and tennis courts, free disc golf, and many other things just sitting there waiting to be used. You can spend hours outdoors, engaging in exercise, hike, or try other activities all without paying a penny. All you have to do is to find and locate these places.

41. Take public transportation.

Make use of the city transit system if you find any close to you. You can use them when going to work instead of driving your car. It's much cheaper, and you won't have to worry about the extra cost or hassle of parking your car.

42. Make your own cleaning products instead of buying them.

You can make your own laundry detergent; this saves you more money rather than buying outside.

43. Start looking for recipes

What you make at home within just a few minutes is impressive, and it also saves you a ton of money compared to the commercial version.

44. Suggest cheap activities when you are with your family and friends

This is often a difficult task, but you can try many techniques. The first thing you can do is to make some suggestions; this gives you the strength to lead a group on cheaper things. For example, if you manage to convince your friends to go to the park and throw hoops instead of playing golf, these green fees will stay in your pocket.

45. Always ask for some fees to be removed

Whenever you sign up for a service of any kind, and there is a registration fee, ask for their waiver. Sometimes it will be (but not always) - and you will

save money simply by not wanting to
pay exorbitant fees.

www.ingramcontent.com/pod-product-compliance
Lightning Source LLC
Chambersburg PA
CBHW030550220526
45463CB00007B/3049